Ed Sheeran: From Rags to a World-Wide Sensation

Table of Contents

Introduction

Ireland. The mention of the country brings about images such as leprechauns, rainbows, and pots of gold. However, the true images that are brought to the forefront of a person's mind that cannot be duplicated anywhere else—images of emerald green landscapes and deep, rolling seas that stir deep within the soul of a person whether he or she is lucky enough to be Irish or not. Nestled a cool fifty three degrees above the equator and only eight degrees west of the Greenwich meridian, Ireland is full of a tumultuous history full of Druids, Vikings, Christians, and pagans alike. Ireland has also produced some of the most notable people in history such as one of the United States' presidents John Fitzgerald Kennedy and the actor that has joined a long line of men acting in the role of James Bond, Pierce Brosnan. Its lush vegetation is bisected by the Shannon River, which flows through the center of the heart of Ireland. Many notable people in history have Irish ancestry, have emigrated directly from Ireland, or are first generation Americans with Irish parents.

Let us travel 'across the little pond' to England and explore. Crossing the English Channel and coming ashore anywhere on the western part of the country of England, we travel across the country toward Suffolk County. Framlingham, a small village with a rich Anglo-Saxon history, sits within the boundaries of the Suffolk Coastal District in Suffolk, England. As with much of England, this small village has retained much of its historical sites including the Framlingham Castle. Mary Tudor, eldest daughter of King Henry VIII, had her confirmation as Queen of England in this city at the church of St. Michael. Framlingham Castle was built by the Normans in 1148 but later destroyed by King Henry II after the revolt of 1173/1174. Roger Bigod, who was the Earl of Norfolk at the time, rebuilt the castle just a few years later. Having been so close to the shores, Framlingam Castle would become the subject of many battles its youth. Not long after it was rebuilt, King John successfully took the castle in 1216.

King John was the youngest son out of five sons of King Henry II and Eleanor of Aquitaine. At first, he was not expected to inherit a significant amount of property since he was the youngest, but his older brothers led a rebellion against King Henry II which left John Lackland to become the favorite and subsequently the Lord of Ireland in 1177. By the time Richard I assumed the throne, John became a potential heir. Though he attempted his own rebellion against his brother, King Richard, while King Richard was fighting in the Third Crusade, John was proclaimed as king in 1199 upon Richard's death. By the late thirteenth century, the castle had become one of its most lavish castles in the country at the time. King John died from dysentery during late 1216 and the throne of England later went to his son, King Henry III.

By the time the fifteenth and sixteenth centuries came to be, Framlingham became the heart of the estates owned by the Mowbray and Howard families, but later fell to ruin after Theophilus stumbled upon some financial issues causing the estates to be sold to pay off the debt he acquired.

Another feature of the town of Framlingham is known as the St. Michael the Archangel Church of Framlingham. Though bits and pieces of the church were built beforehand, the main part of it was built between 1350 and 1555. The architecture of the church is exquisite according to many historians. It was approximately in the year 1635 that Sir Robert Hitcham bequeathed the entire estate to Pembroke College. To this day, it still contains the tombs of such notables as Thomas Howard, third Duke of Norfolk who was a prominent Tudor politician and was the uncle of Anne Boleyn and Catherine Howard. As a matter of fact, he had a large involvement in arranging the marriages of King Henry VIII with these two women. In addition to Thomas Howard, third Duke of Norfolk, Reverend Nicholas Danforth, Henry Thompson, and Laura Wright, Framlingham, England is home to Edward Christopher Sheeran.

Edward Christopher Sheeran was born February 17, 1991 in Halifax, England. However, he spent the majority of his life in Framlingham, England in Suffolk County. Currently, he is a singer/song writer who performs primarily the following genres: pop, R&B, folk, hip-hop, and acoustic. His parents are John Sheeran and Imogen Lock. He also has one older brother named Matthew. As for Matthew Sheeran, his older brother, he is a composer of music. Musical talent is evident in this family. Currently, he still resides in England and operates as a freelance composer. During his childhood, he also sang in the church choir alongside his brother, Ed. He was touted as a wonderful treble soloist who had an unusually developed operatic voice at a very young age. In school, young Matthew performed in school musicals such as 'Grease' and 'West Side Story'. He is well versed in all genres of music. His studies led him to obtain a music degree from the University of Sussex and won the Thomas Beecham scholarship.

Matthew Sheeran also spent time in Germany and Italy working on his musical training and then picked up his studies in England after his travels completed studying at King's College. While his brother was touring the world playing for screaming teens and pre-teens, Matthew was beginning to earn his commissions in freelance composition.

If one were to look at Edward Sheeran, it would be easy to see that he has strong Irish roots, despite being born in England. As a matter of fact, his father's parents were both from Ireland. His paternal grandfather was from Maghera in County Londonderry and his paternal grandmother was from Gorey in County Wexford.

Maghera, Ireland is a small village in Northern Ireland in County Londonderry. The history of this near-ancient city is quite extensive. It is home to St. Lurach's Church, which dates back to 500 A.D. The church was a focal point of Viking raids that happened in the twelfth and thirteenth centuries. Northern Ireland and the Republic of Ireland have a bloody history. This was especially evident during the 1800's when some of the clashes between Catholics and Protestants were at their worst. The 'Orange Order' is an organization made up of Protestants that was created in 1795. The objective was to promote and defend supremacy of Protestantism. The name was created in honor of William of Orange, a protestant, who won the Battle of the Boyne. It was during that time that these 'Orangemen' burned several homes in Maghera to the ground simply because they were the homes of Catholics. Maghera was also the location of many problems during a time in Irish history known as 'The Troubles'.

'The Troubles' describes the period during the twentieth century in which the conflict between the Catholics and the Protestants began to spill over into other countries that are part of the United Kingdom. Many believe it ended in 1998 with the Belfast Agreement, but there has still been some violence, sporadically, taking place between the two religious factions. Though the opposing sides touted their religious faith as an identifier, the conflict was not one of religion. Rather, the conflict was primarily political. Protestants, who were also known to be loyalists to the crown of England, wanted Ireland to remain within the United Kingdom. Catholics, who were known as unionists, wanted all of Ireland to separate and exist as a stand-alone sovereign state. The origin of the conflict, however, is what brought to light that the opposing sides were segregated by their religious beliefs. The conflict was brought about due to discrimination of Catholics by a largely Protestant government as well as internment, or the illegal detaining of those without a fair trial.

Gorey, Ireland is a bit larger than Maghera. It only takes approximately an hour to drive from Dublin, Ireland to Gorey. Gorey, though located within the Republic of Ireland in County Wexford, is also a city filled with many devout Catholics. Though Gorey has not seen the level of bloodshed that Maghera has seen, it still has its own rich history. County Wexford is full of Viking history. In fact, the Viking name for Wexford is 'Waesfjord'. Translated from Old Norse to English, that roughly translates to 'fjord of mud'. This area has shown evidence of inhabitants from as far back as the Mesolithic period, which took place just after the Ice Age. Fast forward to approximately the fifth century and one can find evidence of the last Irish king of Leinster—Dermot MacMurrough. Beginning in 819, though, Vikings began making a trek to Ireland and landed in Wexford. Over the next sixty years, the Vikings simply plundered, pillaged, and then simply returned home. However, around the latter part of the 800's, the Vikings began settling and creating towns on the shores of Wexford County.

Three hundred years later in 1169, the Normans began their invasion of Ireland. It was in that same year that Robert Fitz-Stephen, in which 'Fitz' means 'son of', led his army of Normans to Bannow Island. It was after battles raged for a few years that the kingdom of Ireland passed to Richard de Clare who submitted to the King of England and subsequently gave lands to those who followed him in feudal traditions. Gorey was part of the landscape that witnessed events in Irish history such as the existence of the Knights Templar, Gaelic resurgence, war between tenants and the English Lords, penal laws against Catholics, and most recently a rebellion of Irish rebels in 1916 just as World War I was getting underway.

His Home Life

Ed Sheeran is well aware of his roots and the history of his family's home—of both Ireland and England— where he grew up. His childhood was normal. He even participated in his church's choir from the age of four! He achieved his high school education at Thomas Mills High School in Framlingham. It was during that time which Ed began truly discovering some of his favorite artists such as: Van Morrison, Damien Rice, The Beatles, Bob Dylan, and Nizlopi. Most people are familiar with Van Morrison, The Beatles, and Bob Dylan. However, Damien Rice and Nizlopi are quite popular among Irish music channels. While Damien Rice is more of a folk/folk rock singer, Nizlopi is a folk/hip-hop musician, though both have had an effect on Ed Sheeran's musical style.

Ed Sheeran firmly supports the arts as he was accepted into the National Youth Theatre in London as a teenager. He is a patron of the Youth Musical Theatre in the UK now. With his size ten shoes and his orange cat named 'Bellini', Ed has known what 'rock bottom' feels like as well as 'cloud nine'. He is the second cousin to the seventy-year-old broadcaster Gordon Burns. He currently has two tattoos—one of a ketchup bottle and the other of a teacup. He does share the same birthday with Paris Hilton, but assures his public that the two are nothing alike. Since his signing with Atlantic Records to present day, his Twitter account, @edsheeran, has accumulated over six million followers, though he only follows a mere five hundred and five Twitter pages. He insists on managing his own Twitter. He has also sent out twenty six thousand tweets of his own. His website, EdSheeran.com, attests to just as many if not more site visits.

Ed's mother, Imogen Lock was a culture publicist along with her husband, John Sheeran. The pair ran an independent art consulting firm called, *Sheeran Lock* for twenty years between 1990 and 2010. Afterwards, his mother became a jewelry designer. Currently, her jewelry highlights and sells on Ed Sheeran's website. Along with his mother's jewelry, he also has available an orange vinyl version of his album '(+)' on his website. His father, John, still lectures on art and art culture at various locations throughout England, Ireland, and the rest of the United Kingdom. Another interesting thing about Ed Sheeran's parents are that both are completely deaf. He grew up using British Sign Language and is now fluent in it. He also supports the deaf community and even had a sign language interpreter sign during the entire production of one of his videos.

When asked what it is like to grow up in a deaf family, Ed Sheeran has one of the world's most simple answers available—no different from being in a family that can hear. The only major difference is in handling the telephone or translating for those who cannot sign. The thing that resonated within his thoughts was that while people ask questions about his childhood, the reason is not to pry. The reason is simply that that person finds it interesting. As children, we are taught that the only 'dumb question' is a question that goes unasked. That, coupled with our natural inquisitiveness and curiosity, makes for a sometimes socially awkward position. Questions about one's life and the differences between our lives do not always come from a desire to mock or psychoanalyze a person— they come from genuine interest. Ed Sheeran has always taken an offensive approach rather than defensive approach while happily answering questions to educate those who are not aware of what it takes with his unique position of existing in both worlds—the world of the hearing and the world of the deaf.

Young Ed Sheeran also grew up a victim of bullying, so he knows exactly what it is like for today's children. Bullying is no fun. Often, it is more than simple teasing. Bullying is truly the intentional emotional abuse of one person of another. The objective of the bullying is often to elicit an emotional response from the target—often crying or running away. Ed Sheeran grew up with his signature red hair, thick glasses, and he stuttered. Though he is not deaf like his parents, he did have some minor hearing problems of which he eventually outgrew. He often tells people that he did blossom into a successful young man, and that is what is important. He feels that the teasing and bullying is part of what made him who he is today. Another thing that he has noticed is that those who bullied him as a child are now being 'bullied' by life, in a sense. He notes that most of them are seemingly 'stuck' in their own mundane lives with no true sense of what is out there in the world just waiting on them to grab it.

His Natural Passion

Sheeran always had a natural inclination and love for music. Apparently, it ran in the family as his older brother, Matthew, is a composer. In addition to that, his two younger brothers are post-graduate music students. Ed's first guitar was given to him as a gift by his uncle, but he did not have formal music lessons until later. He reportedly tells interviewers that he gives all of his guitars male names such as the following: Nigel, Cyril, Felix, Lloyd, James, and Trevor. Though guitar is his primary instrument and instrument of preference, he can also play the bass, cello, and piano. A little known fact is that he also can speak other languages such as German and Greek.

Ed has reportedly told interviewers that he admires his father. The two have always had a close relationship. If the pair were to be placed side by side, the resemblance between the two is uncanny. Yet, life was not always so smooth for young Ed. Though he was close to his parents and grandparents, he had a wild streak—quite rebellious. His parents raised him in a fairly strict home, severely limiting the amount of time he spent in front of the television and refused to even purchase an electronic gaming system. He reportedly said that while his friends on the tour bus are playing with the X-box, he has to refrain as he does not know what to do with the thing. In 2008, Ed moved to London at the age of seventeen, leaving his parents' home. He stayed with friends and even slept at a location called the 'Underground' where most of London's homeless sleep. He did this during the time he spent trying to break into the music industry.

While he was being interviewed by DailyMail of England, he was asked about his contact list in his telephone. The reporter joked about it being full of the 'who's who' of show business, but the most interesting thing about his contact list was the fact it contained Courtney Cox's phone number. Many wondered how the young man came to know Cox since he was not allowed a lot of television time. Ed describes the situation as an interesting one as he was invited to a party at the cousin of a friend of his. That cousin happened to be Courtney Cox. Ed tells DailyMail that Courtney Cox is very down-to-Earth and normal. He does believe that the fact she's from Alabama might have something to do with her genuine friendliness as the southern United States is known for being the 'Home of Hospitality and Grace'.

In the same interview, Ed details his childhood, struggles, and how he went from being homeless to being a superstar. Ed tells the interviewer that he was not homeless in the worst extreme of the word. He did not live in cardboard boxes, but he flitted from couch to couch and sometimes slept on the Circle Line, similar to a subway. He also slept at the gates of Buckingham Palace. That experience inspired his song, *Homeless*. One thing is for certain. Despite his struggles with existing on limited means, his sudden fame and fortune have not seemed to have changed him to date. He says that he still does what many people his age do—drink tea from bowls rather than cups and existing on a diet of Ramen noodles. Well, it is not quite to that level, but most people get the point. He does not dine out for every meal and flaunt his earnings. Rather, he spends it mostly investing in property—something that will outlast him.

Every person who travels has a favorite place that he or she has visited. Those who have been unable to fulfill their desires for travel have a place they have fantasized about often. For Ed Sheeran, a person who has traveled extensively, his favorite place that he has visited thus far has been Australia. Australia used to be a penal colony for England, but over time has become a very well-known place of culture. He prefers Australia because of its vast cultural locations, and it fits with his inner 'need' for exploration.

The Beginnings of His Career

The first of his records to be released happened in 2005 when he was just fifteen years old. The title of this record was *The Orange Room*. The four tracks that are featured on this EP are: 'I Love You', 'Addicted', 'Misery', and 'Moody Ballad of Ed'. This record did really well and propelled him on the fast track to fame. That fast track did take three years, but it was what got his name and talent recognized. It was in 2008 that he moved back to London to truly begin his music career. He played in all sorts of smaller venues and sometimes performed in small five-person groups. It was also around that time that he opened for Nizlopi, one of his favorite bands well known for their track 'The JCB Song'.

The year 2008 was a year that Ed Sheeran attempted to expand his repertoire. He decided to try his hand at acting by auditioning for a television series called *Britannia High*. This series is a drama that takes place at a fictional London theater house. One group of teenagers who attend school at this theater house interact with one another in a drama. Ed Sheeran, along with another individual named Danielle Peazer. Both were turned down for the parts. As it turns out, their denial for parts was not a bad thing as the show later tanked with horrible ratings.

That following year, he released another EP titled, *You Need Me*. It was well-favored by those that knew him and caused him to be more recognized in the music industry. His notoriety had spread through the country so much that it was noted he performed an astonishing total of three hundred and twelve gigs that year. He even toured with the British musician, 'Just Jack'.

The next year, in 2010, he released a total of four EP's beginning with 'Let It Out' followed by 'Loose Change'. The second one contained the song that set him on track as his own artist titled, *The A Team*. The music video for this song cost a mere £20 to film and produce, and features a cameo of the artist. The third EP was a collection of tracks he wrote in tandem with another artist and friend by the name of Amy Wadge. That same year, he also went on tour with a band called *Example*.

In addition to touring with *Example*, he also performed at various open mic nights in Los Angeles, California during his tour in the United States.

During one of these open mic nights in Los Angeles, California, Jamie Foxx saw him perform and really liked what he was hearing from this red-haired British singer. Jamie Foxx is a comedian, actor, and a musician himself and even played the role of Ray Charles in the movie titled, *Ray*. Since Jamie Foxx enjoyed Ed Sheeran's work so much, he offered Ed an opportunity to use Foxx's recording studio.

His final independent EP produced by himself titled, 'Number 5 Collaborations Project' and featured artists such as Devlin, Wiley, JME, and Wretch 32. Featuring other British artists, it rose to position forty-nine on the United Kingdom Album Charts. Once he realized his music career was finally producing some success, he put on a free show in Camden, England as a way to thank his fans for their support. Since over one thousand people turned up for the first one, he put on four more free shows just to make sure that everyone had an opportunity to watch. This led to him signing a deal with Atlantic Records. His music career had finally succeeded making his dreams of performing a reality.

His First Major Hit

Just a few weeks after signing with Atlantic Records, 'The A Team' was re-released on his debut track. It managed to earn spot number three on the United Kingdom Singles Chart, and sold over fifty-eight thousand copies becoming the eighth best-selling single track of the year in England. He also performed the track on the television show, 'Later…with Jules Holland'. His next single charted at the number four spot.

His next album, (+), sold over one hundred thousand copies in the first week of its release and topped the charts in the United Kingdom. His music career had truly taken a major turn for the better, especially after his next single's music video managed to snag an appearance from Rupert Grint (Harry Potter) as an obsessed fan. His next video featured Nina Nesbitt who also toured with him.

To date, Ed Sheeran has released four studio albums, eleven EP's, ten singles, and twelve music videos. He began as an indie musician in 2005. For six years, he did his own marketing, arranged his own performances, produced his own records, and wrote his own songs.

One of Sheeran's most prolific songs, however, was a tribute to miscarriages. *Small Bump* was the next single to top the charts. It was quite the tearjerker, but brought light to what those who have suffered a miscarriage endure in that process.

Sheeran is not immune from gossip mongering or paparazzi. Many tabloids have suggested that he has paired with Taylor Swift, though the two are only strong friends. In fact, he recorded a duet with her titled, *Everything Has Changed*. This duet is to be released on Taylor Swift's next single.

Not only has Sheeran contributed to Taylor Swift's career, but he has also contributed to One Direction's second album. The song he wrote titled *Little Things* topped the United Kingdom's Singles Chart. His assistance to other bands and artists did not cease with Taylor Swift and

One Direction. He also extended his talents to Wretch 32 in *Hush Little Baby* and Devlin's *WatchTower*.

The year 2012 was a big year for Sheeran as well. He provided support to Snow Patrol on their United States tour as well as performed for the Queen's Diamond Jubilee, performed a cover of *Wish You Were Here* by Pink Floyd at the Summer Olympics in London during closing ceremonies, and won two BRIT awards. His first award was for the 'Best Breakthrough Act' and the next one was for 'Best Solo Male Artist'. He also was awarded for 'Best Song Musically and lyrically' in the 2012 Ivor Novellos, and later performed a duet with Elton John.

In addition to reaching a top-level musician status in England and the United States, he tops many different charts in Ireland, New Zealand, and Australia as well as Canada. His most popular album, (+), has been certified as a five-time platinum which means it has sold over one-and-a-half million copies across the United Kingdom.

His manager, Stuart Camp, constantly praises Ed Sheeran's huge heart. Most likely, his kind and gentle nature stems from the fact that he had a positive upbringing. In addition to how he was raised, he has also been in situations where he has had to depend on the kindness of others—often having to crash on the couches of friends. The two charities he contributes to are Crisis and Bluebell Wood Children's Hospice.

Crisis is a charity that helps those who are homeless in the United Kingdom, but more specifically, they help *single* homeless people—a situation which Ed Sheeran is all too familiar. Crisis has invested over forty years' worth of time in trying to help those who tend to fall through the cracks of the system. They have acquired many statistical data on single person homelessness, 'rough sleeping', squatting, and the physical and mental health of those who live in such conditions.

Rough sleeping is just another term for someone who literally sleeps on the streets due to having absolutely nowhere else to go for the night. Most homeless shelters dedicate themselves to veterans, families, or battered women as well as children. There are very few shelters dedicated to those who are single, homeless, and without children. The few that are in existence often fill up too quickly and require a sort of waiting list. Due to involvement of non-profit agencies such as Crisis, the numbers in England dropped from almost two thousand people sleeping on the streets in 1998 to barely five hundred people sleeping 'rough' in 2002.

Single and hidden homelessness is something Ed Sheeran experienced pre-stardom. 'Hidden' homelessness usually describes those who have no place of their own but drift from place to place and couch to couch as a transient and sometimes become squatters. 'Squatting' usually entails the act of residing temporarily in an abandoned shelter or something similar.

Tons of statistical data exists on the physical and mental health issues that the homeless face due to their circumstances. Sometimes, though, homelessness traces its cause to the mental state of the individual. Often, schizophrenics and those with similar afflictions find themselves homeless if they do not find themselves placed in a mental facility first.

The physical maladies afflicting the homeless often reduce one's life expectancy by an average of thirty years. In their report titled, *Still Dying for a Home*, many of those interviewed attribute the early deaths to various reasons such as the following: hypothermia, suicide, murder, and various health maladies that could have otherwise been easily treated had they had the means to procure said treatment. Many of those interviewed stated that it made them reflect upon their own lives and current situation. The funerals for the homeless are often a sad sight as well. Friends and family of the deceased often attend most funerals, but those of the single and one or two people— if anyone at all attend homeless. Many homeless are buried in unmarked graves.

In this comprehensive report, the question is asked as to how their life could be improved. The answers are simple. Most simply want a place to live and support of family. Most people are taught in childhood that a family bond is unbreakable. However, the practice of that teaching is often found to be a great disappointment.

With regard to mental illness, it appears as if mental illness is almost a pre-requisite for homelessness. It goes right along with drug and alcohol use. Drugs and alcohol are often used to 'self-medicate' the depression associated with not having a home or place to sleep. Maslow's hierarchy of needs explains how if one's basic needs are not met (shelter, food, security), one can often spiral into a mental illness.

Research indicates that it takes an individual approximately three weeks to adapt to being homeless, but even longer to acclimate to mainstream society if the person is even able to do so in the first place. The mental health issues often pose the biggest risk to those living on the streets.

His Free Time

It is quite evident to see why Ed Sheeran donates frequently as well as volunteers his time to this cause—he has been among them and could have easily been a statistic had his music career not been successful. As a matter of fact, he participated in the 2011 campaign called 'No One Turned Away' that fought against proposed budget cuts to the funding that supported Crisis.

Another one of his philanthropies is the Bluebell Wood Children's Hospice. A hospice is a facility that offers services to those who have terminal illnesses. The Bluebell Wood Children's Hospice specifically targets helping children who happen to find themselves in this predicament along with their families. It is similar to St. Jude's Hospital in the United States. In the United Kingdom, Bluebell Wood Children's Hospice opened in 2008. If one were to look at their website, that person would see tons of stories like a child named Richard who had not only a rare, terminal illness but also developed cancer. Bluebell Wood Children's Hospice saw to it that Richard was able to pass away in the comfort of his own home rather than in the sterile surroundings of a hospital. The facility rests on just over six acres and has top-of-the-line accommodations that make the remaining days of these terminal children and their families as pleasant as possible during the most trying times of their lives.

Ed Sheeran also donates time and money to this worthy cause. He even managed to visit one of the residents there in order to fulfill her dying wish. This young woman, Katie Papworth, was a huge fan of Sheeran. She even proposed to Sheeran while presenting him with some of her artwork before her aggressive brain cancer took away her sight. Despite his fame and fortune, he has never been too proud to stop his schedule and take care of the needs of his fans who need him the most. His presence and humble attitude can often brighten anyone's day. Yet, he is not alone in his attempt to alleviate the pain of those who suffer. One Direction's Lucas Tomlinson, Howard Webb, and Sara Stevenson all join with Sheeran as one of the hospice's biggest contributors of time and money.

Ed Sheeran also donates his time and money to programs that reach out to prostitutes in the United Kingdom. He has performed gigs in places such as Bristol and raised thousands of dollars for these charities. He says that often the people who sell themselves on the streets are looked upon with trash and are considered by society to be disposable people, but there are reasons people find themselves turning to prostitution. Sheeran believes that prostitutes deserve the same help that anyone else deserves, if not more. The campaign that helped to raise awareness and money for the charities that help prostitutes was called 'Give It Up for One Twenty Five'. The objective was to encourage people to give up something for one hundred and twenty five hours.

His most recent philanthropy is called 'Band Aid 30'. 'Band Aid 30' is a mega-charity that worked to stop the spread of Ebola during the scare this past year in 2014. Ebola is a very deadly virus that causes people to hemorrhage internally. The problem is that you cannot touch a person with Ebola to comfort them. This is particularly unfortunate, as it has been scientifically proven that the sense of touch can vastly improve a person's ability to heal from a disease or injury.

When he is not whirling around the globe and visiting dying fans, Ed Sheeran likes to relax on his property in Tennessee. He bought the property in Nashville, Tennessee in 2013. The reason for the move is that he wanted to live somewhere known for its music. What better place in the world than Nashville, Tennessee—home to country music, the Grand Ol' Opry, and Elvis Presley? However, Nashville is no longer home to country stars alone. People such as Jack White, The Black Keys, and Sheryl Crow have made 'music city' home. One of his favorite things about Nashville, Tennessee—there are no paparazzi wandering the streets as with other cities teeming with celebrities. He also compares Nashville, Tennessee to his home in Framlingham, England citing that the two are very similar in the rural qualities that he adored about his home.

Sheeran also owns a farm that exists near his hometown. He has stated that he hopes to raise a family there eventually, but knows that right now is not his time to settle down with a family. His feelings on the subject are that it would not be fair to the woman he settled down with or the children he may have to have him gone on tours all the time. That is the primary reason he is being very cautious with this earnings.

Ed Sheeran has made many tours across the globe. For 2015, his tour includes such countries as The United Arab Emirates, Qatar, China, South Korea, China, The Philippines, Singapore, and Malaysia. Of all of the songs Ed has written and performed, he tells reporters and interviewers that 'Give Me Love' is his favorite one to perform. The meaning behind the song is not what one would think, though. Ed Sheeran wrote the song while sitting in a garden behind a friend's shed and wanted a low-key soulful feel to it.

In 2011, Ed participated along with several other artists in 'The Collective' and performed the cover song, 'Teardrops' which was originally performed and written by a band called 'Massive Attack'. The performance was to raise money for 'Children in Need'. 'Children in Need' is a program designed to help disadvantaged youth across the United Kingdom. His philanthropy does not stop there. Though he contributes to several other charities, either through a donation of time or money, he officially is affiliated with three primary charities: ONE Campaign, GRAMMY Foundation, and Musicians on Call.

ONE Campaign is a charity designed to get Americans involved with the AIDS epidemic and poverty. AIDS, or Acquired Immunodeficiency Syndrome, is a virus that wreaks havoc on a person's immune system. The disease weakens the immune system by attacking the T-cells that attack viruses and bacteria thus making the individual more susceptible to infections such as pneumocystis pneumonia, Kaposi's sarcoma, and other opportunistic infections. Scientists in the United States of America first discovered the existence of the virus in 1981, though the disease did not officially earn the moniker of AIDS until the following year. The origins were traced to primates in Africa.

One Campaign not only seeks to erase the stigma and discrimination against those with the disease, it seeks to find a cure. Since the disease was first discovered, many people with the disease often were forced into a social isolation. Many people feared catching the virus through casual contact such as a handshake. In fact, one young child by the name of Ryan White was portrayed in media due to the discrimination he suffered once it was discovered he had the disease. Though the common misconception of the time was that only drug addicts or homosexuals contracted the virus, Ryan White was a hemophiliac—meaning he required multiple blood transfusions over his lifetime. Unfortunately, one of these transfusions led to him getting the virus. The result was that his case did lead to blood donations being screened for diseases. His case was typical for that time. The discrimination White suffered was that his school expelled him due to his infection. Doctors did tell the school board that the boy was not a threat to other students and his disease posed no risk. However, due to lack of understanding of the disease, parents and teachers fought against his attendance.

Other celebrities who support the ONE Campaign are Kellan Lutz (Twilight), Annie Lennox (musician), and Bono (musician) along with many more. Ed, however, has not only taken with the fight against AIDS, but also the war on poverty for which ONE Campaign raises money.

Ed Sheeran also takes part in the GRAMMY Foundation. Many schools across the United States of America often face budget cuts. More often than not, the first programs cut are music and art. The GRAMMY Foundation was created in 1988 that sought to educate people and gain an understanding as well as appreciation for music and the arts by emphasizing the impact it has on American culture.

Musicians on Call is a program that connects musicians with their fans in one of the most unusual places—the hospital. There are individuals out there who are forced to live in medical residential facilities and do not have the opportunity to attend concerts or keep up with the latest music releases from their favorite artists—something most of the general population takes for granted.

Founded in New York City, New York, Musicians on call was created to help bring music to those stuck in these facilities. According to the information on the internet, it has provided these services to over seventy thousand patients at various hospitals. It is also linked to another program called 'Project Playback'. Many of the artists who participate in both programs all say the same thing—they failed to realize prior to their involvement in either of these programs just how much music affects people and brings them to life during a time when that person is staring death in the face. Ed Sheeran has participated in Musicians on Call. One of his performances raised over twenty two thousand dollars for the charity.

July 8, 2013, one of the radio stations in Nashville, Tennessee hosted what it called the 'STAR PARTY' at one of the local restaurants— the Hard Rock Café. Every single dollar from the proceeds went toward Musicians On Call charity. The amount raised was enough to fund the charity for a year.

The crowd gave Ed Sheeran a standing ovation for his performance. At the time of his performance, he was touring with Taylor Swift during the North American RED Tour. The North American RED Tour was launched to promote her new album and her friend, Ed Sheeran, was more than willing to support her in that.

Concerning the concerts, the 'STAR PARTY' also held auctions (both live and online) which gave out different memorabilia from various stars such as the following: The Black Keys, Kelly Clarkson, Gene Simmons, Darius Rucker, Keith Urban, and many other well-known artists.

As with many artists and celebrities, the public often wants to know whom that person has been linked to romantically. One of these women that has had the experience many young 'fan girls' crave is Ellie Goulding.

 Goulding was born in 1986 on December 30th. She is from England and like Sheeran, she plays many instruments and her career is defined as being a singer and songwriter. After Jamie Lillywhite discovered her, she signed with Polydor Records.

It was just the following year of her signing with Polydor Records that in 2010, she topped the BBC's poll of the top British artists. In addition to that, her newly released album titled Lights hit the charts at the number one spot and sold nearly one million copies. Her success also earned her the opportunity to sing at Prince William's wedding reception at Buckingham Palace.

Her biggest hobby is running. She runs an average of five to six miles every day and is currently training for a marathon. Some of her friends include artists such as Lorde and Katy Perry. She met Ed Sheeran at one of Hollywood's social events and described him as a 'nice guy'. The two dated under the radar, but their break-up was the typical Hollywood cryptic break-up. One of Ed's songs, as a matter of fact, was written about the break-up which was caused by the fact that the tall, leggy blonde cheated on Ed with Niall Horan of One Direction. Ed states in many interviews, after admitting that the source of his song titled *Don't* was written about the affair, that he has since forgiven both Niall and Ellie. Beyond that, Ed does not comment on the event as he lives by the 'gentlemen do not kiss and tell' golden rule of relationships.

Another one of music industry's stars that Ed has been rumored to have dated was Taylor Swift. In many interviews, he dispels the rumors. The two sincerely are just friends, though Ed is flattered at the prospect that many people believe he is 'stud enough' to be believed to be dating Taylor Swift. During one particular interview with *Elle* magazine, he not only discusses his lack of intimate relationship with Taylor Swift but also makes a snarky comment concerning the loss of his virginity being less memorable than selling out at Madison Square Garden three times.

Though he has been linked briefly to only a couple other women in the music and entertainment business, his most recent relationship is with a woman named Athina Andrelos. As of November 2014, the pair had been dating for approximately ten months. They met due to her job as a tour manager for a young lady that opened for Ed during one of his shows. She is no longer working in the music industry. She is now working as a chef under Jamie Oliver. Not much is known about the twenty three year old woman of Greek descent other than she is a huge fan of pugs, and she is the inspiration for his song titled, *Thinking Out Loud*. Not only that, but she also has musical talent.

Ed's entire discography is as such: *The Orange Room (2005), You Need Me (2009), Loose Change (2010), Songs I Wrote with Amy (2010), Live at the Bedford (2010), Number 5 Collaborations Project (2011), One Take (2011), iTunes Festival: London (2011), Thank You (2011), The*

Slumdon Bridge (2012), and iTunes Festival 2012 (2012). Those were the extended plays released over his career to date, but there are a few more singles released in which he was the primary artist. In 2011, he released the following singles: *The A Team, You Need Me I Don't Need You,* and *Lego House.* The next year in 2012, *Drunk, Small Bump,* and *Give Me Love* came out. The year 2013 did not have as many singles released as previous years as he only released the one single titled, *I See Fire.* However, in 2014, Sheeran picked up speed by releasing the following singles: *Sing, Don't, Thinking Out Loud,* and *Make It Rain.* So far this year, he has only released one single titled *BloodStream.*

Though these songs are not the only ones released by Ed Sheeran, they are the ones he has released where he is the primary artist. He has been featured in singles from other artists as well as in music videos.

In closing, Ed Sheeran is a young artist, and that statement is not only referring to his age. His ancestry is Irish and English, but he gives of the 'All American boy next door' vibe. He has many wonderful personality qualities such as humility and gentleness. He has been at the very bottom living in substandard conditions on the street in 'rough' conditions, and he has been at the top of his game with only upwards to go. If Jamie Foxx not ran across him and offered his couch to the red-haired Brit, there is no telling where Ed Sheeran would be now. It is safe to say that his talent would have eventually got him noticed by someone at some point, but it is all in the timing. Timing is everything when one seeks to follow his or her dreams. From the tiny age of four years old, Ed Sheeran knew deep in his soul that music was his path. Though it took a lot of hard work and his failures have been numerous, his successes have outweighed those failures allowing him to push forward. In order to 'pay it forward', he has used his success and fame to benefit others rather than only himself.

Printed in the USA
CPSIA information can be obtained
at www.ICGtesting.com
LVHW010228021023
759871LV00019B/370